Pharmacy Technician Exam Review by Sharon D. Garrett, CPhT

Published by Sharon Denise Garrett, CPhT
Harvey, LA, 70058
gpsrxla@gmail.com

Copyright © 2022 Sharon Denise Garrett
First Edition

Cover by Canva

Disclaimer notice:

Please note the information contained within this document is for educational and entertainment purposes only. All efforts have been executed to present accurate, up to date, reliable, and complete information. No warranties of any kind are declared or implied. Readers acknowledge that the author is not engaging in rendering of legal, financial, medical, or professional advice. The content within this book has been derived from various sources. Please consult a licensed professional before attempting any techniques outlined in this book.

By reading this document, the reader agrees that under no circumstances is the author responsible for any losses, direct or indirect, which are incurred as a result of the use of the information contained within this document, including, but not limited to, --- errors, omissions, or inaccuracies.

D1710998

Table of Content

Sig Codes & Abbreviations

AA or AAA	Apply to the affected area
ac	Before meals
ad	Right ear
ADD	Attention Deficit Disorder
ADE	Adverse Drug Effect
ADHD	Attention Deficit Hyperactivity Disorder
ADR	Adverse Drug Reaction
Ag or AG	Silver
AIDS	Acquired Immune Deficiency Syndrome
AM or am	Morning
amp	ampule
amt	amount
APAP	Acetaminophen
aqua	water
AS	Left ear
ASA	Aspirin
ASAP	As soon as possible
AU	Both ears
AWP	Average Wholesale Price
bid	Twice daily
BM	Bowel movement
BP	Blood pressure
BS	Blood sugar
BSA	Body surface area

Sig Codes & Abbreviations

c	with
Ca	calcium
caps	capsules
Cc= ml or mL	Cubic centimeter/ milliliter
CHF	Congestive heart failure
Cl	Chloride/chlorine
cm	centimeter
conc	concentration
Cu	Copper
DAW	Dispense as written
dil	dilute
disp	dispense
DS	Double strength
D_W	Dextrose (somebody %) in Water (D5W= dextrose 5% in water)
DUR	Drug Utilization Review
dx	diagnosis
EC	Enteric coated
Elix.	elixir
FDA	Food and Drug Administration
Fe	Iron
Fl oz	Fluid ounce
G or gm	Gram
GI	Gastrointestinal
gr	Grain
gtt	drop

Sig Codes & Abbreviations

H or hr.	hour
Half Normal	0.45% Sodium Chloride (0.45gm/100ml)
hs	bedtime
H20	water
H2O2	Hydrogen peroxide
HA	headache
HCTZ	hydrochlorothiazide
HIV	Human Immunodeficiency Virus
HMO	Health Maintenance Organization
hx	history
ID	Intradermal (skin)
ien	In each nostril
IM	Intramuscular (muscle)
Inh	Inhale or inhalation
Inj	Inject or Injection
IT	Intrathecal (spine)
IV	Intravenous (vein)
IVPB	Intravenous piggyback
K	Potassium
KCl	Potassium Chloride
kg	Kilogram (2.2 lbs.) or (1000 gm)
L (liquid volume)	Liter (1000 ml)
L (roman numeral)	50
lb	Pound (1 kg) or (16 oz)
liq	liquid

Sig Codes & Abbreviations

mcg	Microgram
MDI	Metered dose inhaler
mEq	milliequivalent
mg	Milligram (1000 mcg)
MgSO4	Magnesium Sulfate
ML or mL	Milliliter
mm	millimeter
MOM	Milk of Magnesia
MVI	Multi-vitamin
N/V	Nausea and vomiting
Na	Sodium
NaCl or NS	Sodium Chloride= Normal Saline= 0.9% (0.9gm/100ml)
NKA	No known allergies
NPO	Nothing by mouth
NRF	No refills
NSAID	Non-Steroidal Anti-Inflammatory Drug
NTG	nitroglycerin
od	Right eye
os	Left eye
oint	ointment
Ophth or Optic	eyes
otic	ears
ou	Both eyes
oz	ounce

Sig Codes & Abbreviations

pc	After meals
PCN	Penicillin
pf	puff
pm	afternoon
po	By mouth
PPO	Preferred Provider Organization
pr	Per rectum
prn	As needed
pv	Per vaginal
Q	Every or quantity
Q_h	Every ____ hour (24 hours divided by this number will determine # of doses per day)
qAm	Every morning
qd	Every day or daily
qh	Every hour
qhs	Every night at bedtime
qid	Four times daily
qMO	Every month
qod	Every other day
qPm	Every afternoon or evening
qs	Quantity sufficient
qsad	Quantity sufficient as directed
qty	quantity
qWK	Every week
Rx	Prescription or treatment

<u>Sig Codes</u> & Abbreviations

S	sulfur
S' (line over the s)	without
SC	Subcutaneous (under the skin)
SL	Sublingual (under the tongue)
SOB	Shortness of breath
Ss (roman numeral)	One-Half (½)
soln	solution
STAT	immediately
Supp.	suppository
Susp.	suspension
Syr.	syrup
T or Tk	take
tab	tablet
tid	Three times daily
tbsp	Tablespoon or tablespoonful (15mL)
top	Topical
tsp	Teaspoon or teaspoonful (5mL)
UAD	Use as directed
UTI	Urinary tract infection
whz	wheezing
Zn	Zinc

Root Words

Arter/o	Artery
Arthr/o	Joint
Bronch/o	Bronchus
Carcin/o	Cancer
Cardi/o	Heart
Cyst/o	Bladder
Derm/o or Derma	Skin
Enter/o	Abdomen
Gastr/o	Stomach
Gluc/o (or) Glyc/o	Sugar
Hem/o	Blood
Hepat/o	Liver
My/o	Muscle
Nas/o (or) Rhin/o	Nose
Nephr/o (or) Ren/o	Kidney
Neur/o	Nerve
Oste/o	Bone
Path/o	Disease
Phleb/o	Vein
Pneum/o (or) Pulm/o	Lungs or Breath
Proct/o	Rectum
Psych/o	Mind
Thromb/o	Blood Clot
Vas/o	Blood Vessel

Common Prefixes

a- (or) an-	without
Ante- (or) pre-	before, in front of
Anti-	oppose
Bio-	living organism
Brady-	slow
Contra-	against
Dia-	complete
Dys- (or) mal-	abnormal
En-	inside of
Ex-	Outside of
Hyper-	too much, high
Hypo-	too little, low
Inter-	between
Intra-	within
Macro-	large, big
Micro-	small, little
Poly-	many, much
Post-	after, behind
Sub-	under, below
Tachy-	fast

Common Suffixes

- ac (or) -al (or) -ic	Pertaining to
-algia	Pain
-ase	Enzyme
-cyte	Cell
-ectomy	Surgical Removal
-emia	Blood Condition
-itis	Inflammation
-logy	Study of
-oma	Tumor
-osis	Condition
-plasty	Surgical Repair
-rrhage	Bursting of blood flow
-rrhea	Flowing discharge
-sclerosis	Hardening
-scopy	Viewing of
-stasis	Control
-uria	Urine

<u>DAW Codes & Meanings</u>

- DAW Code 0: Substitutions Permitted

- DAW Code 1: Physician prefers BRAND NAME ONLY, no substitutions

- DAW Code 2: Patient prefers BRAND NAME ONLY, Doctor permits substitution

- DAW Code 3: Pharmacist prefers BRAND NAME ONLY, Doctc permits substitution

- DAW Code 4: Generic name not available at this pharmacy, brand name dispensed at brand name price

- DAW Code 5: BRAND NAME dispensed at generic name pric

- DAW Code 6: (undefined for insurance company purposes only)

- DAW Code 7: BRAND NAME is mandated by law to be dispensed

- DAW Code 8: Generic name is not commercially available (N Generic has been created)

- DAW Code 9: Physician prefers generic name, Insurance pla prefers BRAND NAME

Drug Stems, Examples, & Indications

Prefix, Root, suffix	Examples (Generic Names)	Drug Class and Indication
-afil	Avanafil; Sildenafil; Tadalafil; Vardenafil	Phosphodiesterase (PDE) inhibitor (Erectile Dysfunction)
-alol	Labetalol Medroxalol	Beta Blocker + Alpha Blocker (HBP)
-asone	Betamethasone; Dexamethasone; Diflorasone; Fluticasone; Mometasone	Corticosteroid (Steroids)
-bicin	Doxorubicin; Epirubicin; Idarubicin; Valrubicin	Antineoplastic, Cytotoxic agent (Chemotherapy)
-bital	Butabarbital; Butalbital; Phenobarbital (C-IV); Secobarbital (C-II)	Barbiturate (sedative)
-caine	Bupivacaine; Lidocaine; Mepivacaine; Prilocaine; Proparacaine	Local Anesthetic (Pain Relief)
cef-, ceph-	Cefaclor; Cefdinir; Cefixime; Cefprozil; Cephalexin	Cephalosporin Antibiotic
-cillin	Amoxicillin; Ampicillin; Dicloxacillin; Nafcillin; Oxacillin	Penicillin Antibiotic

Drug Stems, Examples, & Indications

Prefix, Root, suffix	Examples (Generic Names)	Drug Class and Indication
-conazole	Fluconazole; Ketoconazole; Miconazole; Terconazole; Tioconazole	Antifungal
-cort	Clocortolone; Fludrocortisone; Hydrocortisone	Corticosteroid (Steroid)
-cycline	Demeclocycline; Doxycycline; Minocycline; Tetracycline	Tetracycline Antibiotic
-dazole	Albendazole; Mebendazole; Metronidazole; Tinidazole	Anthelmintic; Antibiotic; Antibacterial
-dipine	Amlodipine; Felodipine; Nifedipine; Nimodipine; Nisoldipine	Calcium Channel Blocker (HBP)
-dronate	Alendronate; Etidronate; Ibandronate; Risedronate	Bisphosphonate; Bone Resorption Inhibitor (Osteoporosis)
-eprazole	Esomeprazole; Omeprazole; Rabeprazole	Proton Pump Inhibitor (PPI) (GERD/Acid Reflux)
-fenac	Bromfenac; Diclofenac; Nepafenac	NSAID (Pain Relief)

Drug Stems, Examples, & Indications

Prefix, Root, suffix	Examples (Generic Names)	Drug Class and Indication
-floxacin	Besifloxacin; Ciprofloxacin; Levofloxacin; Moxifloxacin; Ofloxacin	Quinolone antibiotic (Fluoroquinolone)
-gliptin	Saxagliptin; Sitagliptin; Linagliptin	Antidiabetic; inhibitor of the DPP-4 enzyme (Diabetes)
-glitazone	Pioglitazone; Rosiglitazone; Troglitazone	Antidiabetic; Thiazolidinedione (Diabetes)
-ilol	Carvedilol	Beta Blocker + Alpha Blocker (HBP)
-iramine	Brompheniramine; Chlorpheniramine; Pheniramine	Antihistamine (Hives/Allergies)
-ivir	Oseltamivir; Zanamivir	Antiviral; Anti-flu
-lam	Alprazolam, Trizolam, Midazolam, Remimazolam	Benzodiazepine (Sedative)
-lamide	Acetazolamide; Brinzolamide; Dorzolamide; Methazolamide	Carbonic Anhydrase Inhibitor (Glaucoma)

Drug Stems, Examples, & Indications

Prefix, Root, suffix	Examples (Generic Names)	Drug Class and Indication
-mab	Adalimumab; Daclizumab; Infliximab; Omalizumab; Trastuzumab	Monoclonal Antibody (Antineoplastic; Chemotherapy)
-mustine	Carmustine; Estramustine; Lomustine; Bendamustine	Alkylating agent (Antineoplastic; Chemotherapy)
-mycin	Azithromycin; Clarithromycin; Clindamycin; Erythromycin	Antibiotic; antibacterial (Macrolides)
-nacin	Darifenacin; Solifenacin	Muscarinic Antagonist (Anticholinergic)
-olol	Atenolol; Metoprolol; Nadolol; Pindolol; Propranolol; Timolol (eye drop)	Beta Blocker (HBP)
-olone	Fluocinolone; Fluorometholone; Prednisolone; Triamcinolone	Corticosteroid (Steroids)
-olone	Nandrolone; Oxandrolone; Oxymetholone	Anabolic Steroid (C-III)
-onide	Budesonide; Ciclesonide; Desonide; Fluocinonide; Halcinonide	Corticosteroid (Steroids)
-osin	Doxazosin, Alfuzosin, Terazosin, Prazosin	Alpha Blockers (Prostate, HBP)

Drug Stems, Examples, & Indications

Prefix, Root, suffix	Examples (Generic Names)	Drug Class and Indication
-ovir	Acyclovir; Famciclovir; Penciclovir; Valacyclovir	Antiviral; Anti-herpes
-ovir	Cidofovir; Ganciclovir; Valganciclovir	Antiviral; Anti- Cytomegalovirus
-pam	Clonazepam; Diazepam; Flurazepam; Lorazepam; Temazepam	Benzodiazepine (Sedative)
-phylline	Aminophylline; Dyphylline; Oxtriphylline; Theophylline	Xanthine Derivative (Bronchodilator- Asthma)
-pramine	Comipramine; Desipramine; Imipramine; Trimipramine	Tricyclic Antidepressant (TCA) (Depression)
-prazole	Dexlansoprazole; Lansoprazole; Pantoprazole	Proton Pump Inhibitor (PPI) (GERD/Acid Reflux)
pred; pred-	Loteprednol; Prednicarbate; Prednisolone; Prednisone	Corticosteroid (Steroids)
-pril	Benazepril; Captopril; Enalapril; Lisinopril; Moexipril; Ramipril	Ace inhibitor (HBP)

Drug Stems, Examples, & Indications

Prefix, Root, suffix	Examples (Generic Names)	Drug Class and Indication
-profen	Fenoprofen; Flurbiprofen; Ibuprofen; Ketoprofen	NSAID (Pain Relief)
-prost	Bimatoprost Latanoprost Travoprost	Prostaglandin Agonist (Glaucoma)
-ridone	Iloperidone; Paliperidone; Risperidone	Aypical Antipsychotic (Bipolar)
-sartan	Candesartan; Irbesartan; Losartan; Olmesartan; Valsartan	Angiotensin II Receptor Blocker; ARBs (HBP)
-semide	Furosemide; Torsemide	Loop Diuretic (Water Pill)
-setron	Alosetron; Dolasetron; Granisetron; Ondansetron; Palonosetron	Serotonin 5-HT3 receptor antagonist, Antiemetic and Antinauseant (Nausea and Vomiting)
-statin	Atorvastatin; Lovastatin; Pitavastatin; Pravastatin; Rosuvastatin; Simvastatin	HMG-CoA reductase inhibitor; Statins (Cholesterol)
sulfa-	Sulfacetamide; Sulfadiazine; Sulfamethoxazole; Sulfasalazine	Antibiotic; Anti-infective; Anti-inflammatory (Sulfonamides)

Drug Stems, Examples, & Indications

Prefix, Root, suffix	Examples (Generic Names)	Drug Class and Indication
-tadine	Cyproheptadine; Desloratadine; Loratadine; Olopatadine (eye drop)	Antihistamine (Allergies)
-tadine	Amantadine; Rimantadine	Antiviral; Anti-influenza A
-terol	Albuterol; Arformoterol; Formoterol; Levalbuterol; Salmeterol	Beta Agonist; (Bronchodilator-Asthma)
-thiazide	Chlorothiazide; Hydrochlorothiazide; Methyclothiazide	Thiazide Diuretic (Water Pill)
-tinib	Crizotinib; Dasatinib; Grlotinib; Gefitinib; Imatinib	Antineoplastic (Kinase Inhibitor) (Chemotherapy)
-trel	Desogestrel; Etonogestrel; Levonorgestrel; Norgestrel	Female Hormone (Progestin) (Birth Control)
tretin-; tretin; -tretin	Acitretin; Alitretinoin; Isotretinoin; Tretinoin	Retinoid; Dermatologic agent; (form of vitamin A) (Acne)

Drug Stems, Examples, & Indications

Prefix, Root, suffix	Examples (Generic Names)	Drug Class and Indication
-triptan	Almotriptan; Eletriptan; Rizatriptan; Sumatriptan; Zolmitriptan	Antimigraine; Selective 5-HT receptor agonist (Migraines)
-tyline	Amitriptyline; Nortriptyline; Protriptyline	Tricyclic Antidepressant (TCA) (Depression)
Vira-; -avir	Abacavir; Efavirenz; Enfuvirtide; Nevirapine; Ritonavir; Tenofovir	Antiviral; anti-HIV
vir; -vir	Adefovir; Entecavir; Ribavirin (along with interferon)	Antiviral; Anti-hepatitis
-vudine	Lamivudine; Stavudine; Telbivudine; Zidovudine	Antiviral; Nucleoside Analogues
-zodone	Nefazodone, Trazodone, Vilazodone	Antidepressant (Depression)
-zolam	Alprazolam; Estazolam; Midazolam; Triazolam	Benzodiazepine (Sedative)
-zosin	aFDAlfuzosin; Doxazosin; Prazosin; Terazosin	Alpha blocker (HBP)

Recalls & Rx Filing Systems

Product Recalls:

- **Class I Recall:** Attempts to notify patients and the public that a drug could cause serious harm or death.

- **Class II Recall:** Pharmacy is notified that a drug has consistency issues with potency. The probability of serious harm is not likely and the effects with the drug may be temporary or reversible. Patient should be monitored.

- **Class III Recall:** Manufacture and pharmacy level only. The public, patient, or pharmacy does not need to be notified. Not likely to cause any serious effects or harm.

Rx Filing Systems:

(Controlled substance inventory must be performed at least once every two years. The records must be kept for at least two years, as well.)

- **Example 1: Two File System (Right hand side):** If a pharmacy wishes to file all controlled substances into one bundle, all the C-III through C-V prescriptions must have a red letter "C" stamped on the lower right-hand corner of the prescription. The second bundle will only contain legend/ non-controlled prescriptions in its bundle.

- **Example 2: Two File System (Left hand side):** If a pharmacy wishes to file C-II controlled substances by themselves, then the C-II prescriptions will be the only prescriptions in the first bundle. Legend/ Non- Controlled prescriptions and C-III through C-V will be in the second bundle. With this system, all the C-III through C-V prescriptions will need a red letter "C" stamped in the lower left-hand corner of the prescription.

- **Example 3: Three File System (No Red Stamps):** When this system, all C-II prescriptions will be in bundle one. All C-III through C-V prescriptions will be in bundle two and legend/non-controlled prescriptions will be in bundle three. There is need to stamp a red letter "C" on the C-III through C-V with this system.

DEA Forms

-DEA Form 41: This form is used to document destruction of controlled substances.

-DEA Form 106: This form is used to report the loss or theft of controlled substances. This form is used only if 5% or more of the total yearly product sold is missing. Example: *If your pharmacy sells 1270 Adderall per year and 64 tablets were to go missing, DEA 106 form must be filled out and submitted by the Pharmacist in Charge (PIC).* If one tablet goes missing, there is no need to fill out this form.

-DEA Form 222: This form is used to purchase and return outdated Schedule II (C-II) drugs only. This form comes available in three colors:

- Blue Copy- The purchaser (Pharmacy) keeps this copy on file for at least two years. The pharmacy is the purchaser until they are returning outdate C-II drugs. When returning C-II drugs, the pharmacy becomes the seller.

- Green Copy- The seller (wholesaler, most times) sends this copy to the local DEA.
- Brown Copy- The seller (wholesaler, most times) keeps this copy on file.

  (*As of October 2019, this form is one piece of paper and is available electronically)

-DEA Form 224: This form is used for a pharmacy to dispense controlled substances and obtain a DEA number.

-DEA Form 225: This form is needed to manufacture and dispense controlled substances. A DEA number is obtained for this purpose.

-DEA Form 363: This form is needed to operate as a controlled substance abuse treatment program or to compound controlled substance medications.

Household Conversions

1 tsp. (teaspoonful)	5 mL	
1 tbsp. (tablespoonful)	15 mL	3 tsps.
1 oz. (ounce)	30mL	2 tbsps. or 6 tsps.
1 cup	240 mL	8 oz. or 16 tbsps. or 48 tsps.
1 pt. (pint)	480 mL	2 cups or 16 oz. or 32 tbsps. or 96 tsps.
1 qt. (quart)	960 mL	2 pts. or 4 cups or 32 oz. or 64 tbsps. or 192 tsps.
1 L (liter)	1000mL	
1 gal (gallon)	3840mL	2 qts. or 4 pts. or 128 oz. or 256 tbsps. or 768 tsps.

Pediatric Dosing Conversion Formulas

- *Fried's Rule Formula: Childs Dose= (Child Age in Months/ 150) x Adult Dose*

EXAMPLE: A pediatric patient has an order for Amoxicillin. The normal adult dose is 250mg q8h. The patient is 12 years old and weighs 104 lbs. Using Fried's rule, how much will the pediatric dose be?

Child Dose= (144 months {this is 12 years x 12 months} / 150) = 0.96

Child Dose= 0.96 x 250 mg

Child Dose= 240mg

The pediatric dose will be 240mg per dose.

- *Young's Rule Formula: Child Dose= (Child Age in Years/ Child Age in Years + 12) x Adult Dose*

EXAMPLE: A pediatric patient has an order for Amoxicillin. The normal adult dose is 250mg q8h. The patient is 12 years old and weighs 104 lbs. Using Fried's rule, how much will the pediatric dose be?

Child Dose= (12 years/ 24 {this is 12 years + 12}) = 0.5

Child Dose= 0.5 x 250 mg

Child Dose= 125mg

The pediatric dose will be 125mg per dose.

- *Clark's Rule Formula: Child Dose= (Child weight in pounds/150) x Adult Dose*

EXAMPLE: A pediatric patient has an order for Amoxicillin. The normal adult dose is 250mg q8h. The patient is 12 years old and weighs 104 lbs. Using Fried's rule, how much will the pediatric dose be?

Child Dose= (104 lbs. /150) = 0.69

Child Dose= 0.69 x 250 mg

Child Dose= 172.5 mg

The pediatric dose will be 172.5mg per dose

<u>Mass Conversions</u>

2.2 lbs. (pounds)	1 kg (kilogram)
1 kg (kilogram)	1000 gm (gram)
1 gm (gram)	1000 mg (milligram)
1 mg (milligram)	1000 mcg (microgram)
1 grain (60 - 65mg)	1 inch (2.54 cm)

<u>*When moving from lbs. To kg, you will divide by 2.2.*</u>

Ex: Convert 330lbs. To kg
330lb / 2.2lbs. per kg (lbs cancel, leaving kg as the only units left)
Answer: 150kg

<u>*When moving from kg. To lbs., you will multiply by 2.2.*</u>

Ex: Convert 56.7 kg To lbs.
56.7 kg x 2.2 lbs. per kg (kg cancel, leaving lbs. as the only units left)
Answer: 124.74 lbs.

<u>How to move between units of Mass:</u>

Kg to gm, multiply by 1000 Ex: 2.5 kg x 1000 = 2500gm	Gm to kg, divide by 1000 Ex: 1750 gm/ 1000 = 17.5kg
Gm to mg, multiply by 1000 Ex: 12.5 gm x 1000 = 1250mg	Mg to gm, divide by 1000 Ex: 500mg/ 1000 = 0.5 gram
Mg to mcg, multiply by 1000 Ex: 100mg x 1000 = 100,000 mcg	Mcg to mg, divide by 1000 Ex: 700 mcg/ 1000 = 0.7mg (this is less than 1mg)

Conversion of Temperatures:

To convert from C* (Celsius) to F* (Fahrenheit), use the formula:

C*= (F - 32) / 1.8

Ex: Convert 150 F* to C*

C*= (150-32) = 118

C*= 118/1.8

C*= 65.6

To convert from F* (Fahrenheit) to C* (Celsius), use the formula:

F*= (C x 1.8) + 32

Ex: Convert 46.4*C to F*

F*= (46.4 x 1.8) = 83.52

F*= 83.52 + 32

F*= 115.52

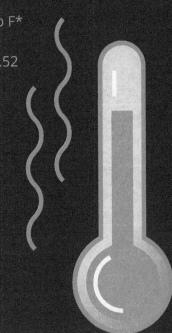

<u>Prescription Criteria & Validating DEA #</u>

Before filling a prescription, you must have the following information:

- Patient Information (Patient name, date of birth, address, & phone number)
- Doctors' Information (Doctor name, correct address, & phone number)
- Date written *(C-II scripts are good for 30 to 90 days, C-III to C-V scripts are good for 6 months, non-controls scripts are for 1 calendar year or 365 days)*
- Drug Name and Strength
- Sig Code (Directions)
- Quantity
- Refills *(C-II scripts has No Refills, C-III to C-V scripts can have a maximum of 5 refills, and non-control scripts can have a maximum of 11 refills)*
- Doctor signature *(and DEA number, if the patient is filling a C-II through C-V prescription)*

All control substance prescriptions need to be verified by the doctor before they are filled. C-II prescriptions cannot be faxed or called in, unless it is a valid emergency. Patient's or patient's caregiver driver license, ID, or passport number must be written on all controlled substance prescriptions.

Prescription Criteria & Validating DEA

With the advancement of technology, a DEA number is verified over a fast and safe internet connection. However, it is still important to understand the basics of how this special number works.

The DEA (Drug Enforcement Agency) assigns medical professionals and hospitals a special number that can keep track of the distribution of controlled substances. _The DEA number contains 2 letters, 6 digits, and 1 check digit._ To prevent drug diversion, misuse, and abuse the following formula was created:

DEA Number: **MG6125341** for **Mikal Garrett, PA (Physician Assistant)**

- The first letter of a DEA Number represents the professional title of the person who is approved to write prescriptions:

A, B, F, or G- _Hospital/ Clinics/ Practitioners (Physicians)/ Teaching Institutions/ Pharmacy_
M- _Mid-level Practitioners (Nurse Practitioners, Physician Assistant's, and Optometrist)_
P or R- _Manufacture/ Distributor, Reverse Distributor (collects expired or unwanted control substances)/ Researcher/ Narcotic Treatment Programs_

Ex: M- For Physician Assistant

- The second letter of a DEA number represents the first letter of the medical professional's last name:

Ex: G for Garrett

Prescription Criteria & Validating DEA

- Step One: Add together the 1st, 3rd, and 5th digits.

  Ex: 6+2+3 = 11

- Step Two: Add together the 2nd, 4th, and 6th digits.

  Ex: 1+5+4 =10

- Step Three: Multiple the sum from step two by 2.

  Ex: 10 x 2= 20

- Step Four: Add the totals from step one and step three together.

  Ex: 11 + 20 = 31

- Step Five: the digit in the ones place from step four should be the same digit as the check digit for your DEA number.

  Ex: 31_ equals MG6125341_

The DEA number MG6125341 is a valid number for Mikal Garrett, PA.

If the digit from step four and the check digit does not match, the umber is invalid, and the controlled substance prescription cannot be filled until the proper medical professional has been contacted.

USP 795, 797, & 800
with IOS Levels

The U.S. Pharmacopeia (USP) is a reference of uniform preparations for the most used drugs that endure multiple tests to ensure their quality, potency and purity are safe for use. A USP Reference Standard (also known as a physical standard) is a known quantity of a drug substance or ingredient, developed in alignment with the specifications outlined.

The International Standards Organization (ISO) aims to ensure that products are safe for patients and healthcare workers. They produce standards that can be incorporated into any size organization regardless of how simple or advanced the production of the products offered must be. ISO levels range from ISO 1(cleanest) to ISO 9 (dirtiest). With regulation standards for ISO combined with USP 795, 797, and 800, Pharmacy Technicians can provide patients with safe drug products.

ISO Level	Air Changes Per Hour	Type of Room or Engineer Equipment inside the area
ISO 9 (Dirtiest)	less than 15	Still cleaner than a regular room environment
ISO 8 (most common)	15-20	• Ante Room of a Hazardous Drug Compounding IV Room (USP 800) • Sterile Hazardous Drug Compounding IV Room (USP 800)
ISO 7 (most common)	30-60	• Ante Room of a Hazardous Drug Compounding IV Room (USP 800) • Sterile Drug Compounding IV Room (USP 797)
ISO 5 (most common)	240-360	Primary Engineering Controls (Laminar Airflow Hood)
ISO 1 (Cleanest)	More than 360	

USP 795, 797, & 800 with IOS Levels

Pharmacy Standards

- **USP 795- Is for non-sterile, non-hazardous, and hazardous drug product compounding.** It can be **a positive or negative pressure room**. It has no ante room, has no ISO level, and each room is equipped with clean work surfaces. *Example of products compounded in the USP 795 standard room: Bulk oral medication and syringes, topical cream, paste, and ointments, immediate use infusions, etc.*

- **USP 797- Is for sterile non-hazardous drug product compounding.** It is an **ISO 7 positive pressure room**. It has an ISO 8 ante room with its own positive pressure. Inside each room there are ISO 5 Primary Engineering Controls (Laminar Airflow Hoods). *Examples of products compounded in the USP 797 standard room: Total Parenteral Nutrition (TPN), antibiotic injections, eye drops, other infusions bags and syringes, etc.*

- **USP 800- Is for sterile category 1 hazardous drug product compounding.** It is an **ISO 8 negative pressure room**. It has an ISO 7 or ISO 8 ante room with positive pressure. Because of the differences in pressure between the clean room and the ante room, USP 800 compounding rooms must have a 2-door system. A 2-door system is where there can only be one entry/exit door open at a time to maintain a safe level of pressure for compounding. If the ante room door (positive pressure) is open, the clean room door (negative pressure) must remain closed until the ante room door is completely closed. Inside each USP 800 room there are ISO 5 Primary Engineering Controls (Biosafety Cabinet (BSC) and Compounding Aseptic Containment Isolator (CACI)) that has its own external ventilation. *Examples of products compounded in the USP 800 standard room: Chemotherapy and other hazardous infusions.*

Storage Temperatures

Refrigeration Temperature: 2*C to 8*C (36*F to 46*F)	Freezer Temperature -50*C to -15*C (-58*F to 5*F)	Room Temperature 20*C to 22*C (68*F to 72*F)
DTaP,Tdap, Td	Cervidil	**Insulin (expires in 28 days)**
DTaP-IPV (Kinrix)	MMR	Inhalers
DTaP-HepB-IPV (Pediarix)	MMRV	Oral Capsules
DTaP-IPV/Hib (Pentacel)	Varicella	Oral Liquids
Hepatitis A	Zoster	Oral Tablets
Hepatitis B	*Coronavirus 19 (Moderna) - 25*C to -15*C	**Tipranavir (HIV) (expires in 2 months)**
HepA-HepB (Twinrix)		Topical Medications
Hib (ActHIB, Hiberix)	*Coronavirus 19 (Pfizer) - 80*C to - 60*C (Deep Freezer)	Transdermal Patches
Hib (PedvaxHIB)		**Xalatan Eye Drops (expires in 6 weeks)**
HPV9 (Gardasil9)		
Influenza (QIV)		
Insulin (All of them)		
Meningococcal (MCV4 – Menactra)		
Meningococcal Group B (Bexsero)		
MMRV		
Pneumococcal (PCV)		
Polio (IPV)		
Rotavirus (RV-1 Rotarix) Tipranavir (HIV medication)		
Xalatan Eye Drops		
*Coronavirus 19 (J&J)		

Retail Basic Math

Retail Prescription Math

Day's Supply= <u>Quantity Dispensed</u>
(Dose X Frequency)

Quantity= Dose X Frequency X Day's

Number of Dose = <u>Quantity Dispensed</u>
Dose

Calculating Eye Drops= 20 gtts/1ml

Day Supply Example:
Rx: Ciprofloxacin 250mg
Take 3 tablets by mouth three times daily
#Disp: 45
DS: Qty/ (Dose X Frequency)
DS: 45 tabs / (3x3) tabs/day
DS: 45 tabs /9 tabs/day (tablets cancel)
DS: 5 days

Quantity:
Rx: Amoxicillin 250 mg
Take 1 tablet by mouth four times daily
for 7 days #QS
Qty: Dose X Frequency X DS
Qty: 1 tab x 4 frequency x 7 days
Qty: 28 tablets

Calculating Eye Drops:
Tobramycin Eye Drop Solution (20 gtts/ml)
#10ml
<u>20 drops</u> = <u>x drops</u>
1ml   10 ml
= 10 ml x 20 drops/ml= 200 drops

Number of Dose:
Gabapentin 300mg #1000/ bottle
How many 900 mg doses are in 1 bottle?
(900 mg/ 300mg per tab= 3 tabs per dose)
Dose: <u>1000 tabs</u>
        3 tabs/dose
Dose: 333.33 doses
Dose: 333 whole doses

PTCB or ExCPT?

Concentrations

Concentration Types:	Expressed As:
W/W	gm/gm
W/V	gm/ml
V/V	ml/ml

(Add like units (gm/gm or ml/ml) for a new total volume)

Percentage Strength for water, creams, paste, sludges, and ointment bases is 0% (zero percent).

To find the final percentage strength, use: $\frac{\text{Active Ingredient}}{\text{Total Volume}} \times 100 = \%$ Strength	To find the active ingredient, use: Total Volume x $\frac{\% \text{ Strength}}{100}$= Active Ingred

- Example: 3gm of active ingredients is mixed with 120 gm of an ointment base. What is the final concentration? (w/w)

  A. 2%   B. 2.4%   C. 3%   D. 2.5%

  3 gm/ (3gm+120gm) = 3gm/123gm = 0.024 x 100 = 2.4%

  Answer: B

- Example: 30gm of active ingredients is mixed with 1000 ml of Normal Saline. What is the final concentration? (w/v)

  A. 30%   B. 3%   C. 0.03%   D. 0.3%

  30 gm/ 1000 ml = 0.03 x 100 = 3%

  Answer: B

- Example: 4 oz of active ingredients is mixed with 500 ml of an alcohol-based solution. What is the final concentration? (v/v)

  A. 24%   B. 0.8%   C. 0.79%   D. 19.35%

  4 oz = 4(30ml) = 120 ml

  120ml / (120 ml + 500ml) = 120ml / 620ml = 0.1935 x 100 = 19.35%

  Answer: D

- Example: How many grams of active ingredients of Miconazole Powder are in 45gm Miconazole 1% cream? (w/w)

  A. 0.45gm   B. 0.0045gm   C. 0.045gm   D. 4.5gm

  45gm x (1/100) = 45gm x 0.01 = 0.45gm

  Answer: A

<u>Dilutions</u>

$$(Q1 \times C1) = (Q2 \times C2)$$

(Q1 = Initial qty	X	C1= Initial conc)	=	(Q2= Final qty	X	C2= Final conc)
(ml or gm)		(% or mg/ml)		(ml or gm)		(% or mg/ml)
(low qty	x	high %)	=	(high qty	x	low %)

1. <u>How much dextrose 50% would be mixed with SWFI to make 5L of dextrose 10%?</u>

      A. 1000ml   B. 1ml   C. 648ml   D. 10ml

5L = 5 (1000ml) = 5000ml
$(Q1 \times 50) = (5000ml \times 10)$
50Q = 50,000
50Q/50 = 50,000/ 50
Q1= 1000 ml
<u>Answer: A</u>

1.2. <u>How much chlorpromazine 100mg/ml should you dilute to prepare 240ml of chlorpromazine 30mg/ml?</u>

      A. 80ml   B. 7.2ml   C. 72ml   D. 8ml

$(Q1 \times 100) = (240 \times 30)$
100Q = 7200
100Q/100 = 7200/ 100
Q= 72ml
<u>Answer: C</u>

1.3. <u>If you dilute 100ml of a 10% solution to 1.5%, how much could you produce?</u>

      A. 1200ml   B. 1500ml   C. 600ml   D. 666.7ml

$(100 \times 10) = (C \times 1.5)$
1000 = 1.5C
1000/ 1.5 = 1.5 C/ 1.5
C= 666.7ml
<u>Answer: D</u>

3+3

Parenteral Calculations

- **Drops per minute:** (Total volume x drip factor) / time in minutes
- **Milliliters per hour:** Total volume in ml / number of hours
- **Infusion Time:** Total volume to be infused in ml / ml per hour to be infused
- **Milligrams per hour:** Total amount of medication in mg/number of hours

Drops per minute: (gtts/min): What is the flow rate to be used to infusion 1500ml of dextrose 5% in water over 5 hours if the drip set delivers 15 drops per ml? (1500ml x 15gtts/ml) = 22,500 gtts 5 hours x 60 mins per hour = 300 mins 22,500gtts / 300 mins = **75 gtts/min**	**Milliliters per hour: (ml/hour):** The pharmacy sent the patient three 1-liter bags. If the infusion lasted 12 hours, how many ml per hour will be infused? 3 x 1L (1000ml) = 3000ml 3000ml/ 12 hours **= 250ml/ hour**
Infusion Time: (hours of time): A patient has an IV that is running 375ml/hr. If the total volume is 2000ml, how many hours will this bag infuse? 2000ml/ 375 ml per hour **= 5.3 hours or 5 whole hours**	**Milligrams per hour (mg/hour):** Ceftriaxone 500mg in 60ml IV syringe to run over 4 hours. How much medication will the patient receive per hour? 500mg/4 hours **= 125mg/ hour**

Drop Factor	Drip Rate (gtts/ml)
60	60 gtts/ml
20	20 gtts/ml
15	15 gtts/ml
10	10 gtts/ml

*Drip Rate: 60 gtts/ml
(this is the standard, unless otherwise noted in the problem)

Medicare Parts and A.D.M.E processes

Medicare Parts:

Medicare is health insurance for individuals over the age of 65 years old, younger people with disabilities, and a person with end-stage renal failure. Medicare is available in four parts:

- **Part A-** Provides hospital insurance for hospital care and treatments
- **Part B-** Provides medical insurance for physicians' visits and medical equipment
- **Part C-** Is called Medicare Advantage and it is a combination of Part A & Part B
- **Part D-** Provides prescription medication insurance
-

Pharmacokinetics:

Pharmacokinetics is how the body handles medications. A.D.M.E. is an acronym for the processes that medications go through once they enter the body.

- **A- Absorption:** how the drug enters the body and bloodstream. For example, pills enter the body through the mouth, oral route of administration. Unlike pills, intravenous injection bypasses the mouth completely. But no matter the route of administration, all medications will end up in the bloodstream.
- **D- Distribution:** how an absorbed medication is transported throughout the body via the circulatory system. Distribution is moving medications from the bloodstream to the body tissues.
- **M- Metabolism:** how medications are inactivated by the "first pass" in the liver (filter system of the body) and attached to specific enzymes to travel to its target.
- **E- Excretion:** how medications leaves the body. Excretion can happen by urine, feces, sweat, and saliva.

Roman Numerals

Roman Numeral	Arabic Number
ss	1/2
I	1
IV	4 (5-1)
V	5
VIII	8 (5+3)
IX	9 (10-1)
X	10
XXX	30 (10+10+10)
XL	40 (50-10)
L	50
LXXX	80 (50+10+10+10)
XC	90 (100-10)
C	100
CD	400 (500-100)
D	500
CM	900 (1000-100)
M	1000

Example: Convert 1970 to Roman Numerals = 1000+900+70

M=1000= M
C-M = (100-1000) = 900= CM
L (50) +X (10) +X (10) = 70= LXX

Answer= MCMLXX

Example: Convert MCMLXXXV to Arabic Number.

1000+ (100-1000) +50+30+5
1000+900+50+30+5= 1985

Answer= 1985

Allegations

Allegation is a method that is used to create a product that is not commercially available using dilution. You are taking a higher percentage concentration product that is low in volume and mixing it with a lower percentage concentration product that is high in volume to create a concentration strength that is found between the high and low percentages that is equal to your total volume.

To identify if the equation you have is an Allegation, you need three of these four things:

- High Percent (H %)
- Low Percent (L %)
- Desired or Wanted Percent (W%) (This number numerically will fall between the high number and low number. If you had a number line, your high and low numbers will be on each end. And your desired or wanted number will fall between your high and low numbers. ALWAYS!!!
- Total Volume (TV must be in mL or gm)

If you have less than three of the four inputs, you probably do not have an Allegation equation.

Example: How many mL of the 15% and 2.5% alcohol-based solution is needed to produce 460ml of a 7.5% alcohol-based solution.

To perform this calculation, use the Tic-Tac-Toe grid to properly set up your equation.

High Percent (H%): 15%		X value- parts of the H% needed: 5
	Desired/ Wanted Percent (W%) 7.5%	
Low Percent (L%) 2.5%		Y value- parts of the L% needed: 7.5

<u>Allegations</u>

- Step 1: Diagonally from top left to lower right, you need to subtract.

  Meaning: H% - W% = Y value or 15 – 7.5 = 7.5

- Step 2: Diagonally from lower left to upper right, you need to subtract.

  Meaning: L% - W% = X value or 2.5 - 7.5 = 5 (there are no negative numbers in allegations)

- Step 3: Vertically on the right side, you need to add.

  Meaning: X value + Y value = Total number of parts needed or 5 + 7.5 = 12.5

- Step 4: Use the formula, <u>X/ (X+Y) * TV</u> to find the volume of the H% that is needed.

  Meaning:

  5 / (5 + 7.5) * 460 ml
  5/12.5* 460ml
  = **184 ml of the 15% alcohol-based solution is needed**

- Step 5: Because we have identified the volume needed for the high percent, now we can subtract that volume from the total volume to find the volume that is needed from the low percent. Use this formula: <u>TV – X volume = Y volume</u>

  Meaning:

  460ml – 184 ml
  = **276 ml of the 2.5% alcohol- based solution is needed**

So you need **184 ml of the 15% alcohol-based solution + 276 ml of the 2.5% alcohol-based solution** to produce <u>460 ml of a 7.5% alcohol-based solution.</u>

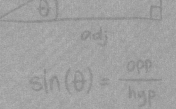

National Drug Code (NDC)

Each drug produced by a manufacturer has a specific identifying NDC number. The NDC number contains three segments of digits, which identifies the manufactures, drug, and pack size. In total, a NDC number contains 11 digits. If a digit is missing in any segment, you can add a leading zero to that segment.

- First Segment – The first 5 digits in a NDC number identifies the manufacturer. All drugs made by the same manufacturer will have the same first 5 digits for all drugs that they manufacture.

*Example: Watson: **62037***

- Second Segment- The next 4 numbers in a NDC number identifies the specific drug made by a manufacturer. Each drug has its own number. Drugs that have the same name, but different strengths, will have the same match first three numbers in this segment.

Example:
*Metoprolol Succinate ER 50mg – **831 or 0831***
*Metoprolol Succinate ER 100mg – **832 or 0832***

- Last Segment- The last two numbers in a NDC number identifies the package size.

Example:
Drugs that come in a quantity of 100 tablets has the identifying number of 01. Drugs that have the quantity of 500 tablets has the identifying number of 05. And drugs that have the quantity of 1000 has the identifying number of 10.

Final:
Waston, Metoprolol Succinate ER 50mg #100 – **62037-0831-01**
Waston, Metoprolol Succinate ER 100mg #1000- **62037-0832-10**

(handwritten: med, size, company)

How shall we store these?

Use the table below, fill in the information that is missing. Use the correct conversion formula to tell me the proper storage temperature.

Drug Brand Name	Generic Name	Where to store?	Temp in F and Temp in C	Refills
1. NitroStat	Nitroglycerin	Room temp	68-77 F 20-25 C	11 refills
2. Lasix				
3.	Dinoprostone Vaginal Suppository			
4. Rocephin				
5. Flu Vaccine				
6. Androgel				
7. Covid Vaccine (Pfizer)				
8. Tylenol #3				
9.	Cefdinir			
10. Amoxicillin (reconstituted)				
11. Xalatan				
12. Concerta				

Practice Exam Questions

1. How many 900 mg doses are available in a 1000 count bottle of 300mg tablets?
A. 100 doses
B. 333 doses
C. 250 doses
D. 334 doses

_____

2. You have a prescription for Naproxen 800mg tablets. #120. How many doses are available if the patient's dose is 1200mg?
A. 60
B. 70
C. 80
D. 90

3. If a patient takes ½ tsp po q6h, they will need 180ml for how many days' supply?
A. 20 days
B. 18 days
C. 16 days
D. 12 days

4. A 16-month-old child needs Tylenol. The normal adult dose is 500 mg. What is the appropriate dose for the child using Fried's Rule?
A. 16 mg
B. 25 mg
C. 6 mg
D. 33 mg

5. A 4 ½ year old needs Amoxicillin. The normal adult dose is 250mg. What is the appropriate dose for the child using Young's Rule?
A. 62 mg
B. 68.2 mg
C. 69 mg
D. 68 mg

6. A child weighs 42kg. How many mg would be appropriate for the child, if the normal adult dose is 500mg using Clark's Rule?
A. 308 mg
B. 414 mg
C. 125 mg
D. 500 mg

7. The recommended dose for Biaxin is 30mg/kg/day divided q8h. How many mg would a 75-pound patient take for each dose?

A. 750 mg
B. 1023 mg
C. 341 mg
D. 1200 mg

8. Prepare 5L of Dextrose using 2000 ml of Dextrose 50% in water mixed with 3000 ml of Dextrose 10% in water. What would be your percentage strength?

A. 35%
B. 26%
C. 25%
D. -25%

9. If you mix 0.75gm of 1% cream with 14.25 gm of a cream base, what would be your percentage strength with a total volume of 15gm?

A. 5%
B. 0.5%
C. 0.05%
D. 5.05%

10. If you mix 480 ml of Dextrose 70% in water with 480 ml of Dextrose 10% in water, what would be your total volume and percentage strength?

A. 960 ml Dextrose 40% in water
B. 840 ml Dextrose 60% in water
C. 480 ml Dextrose 40% in water
D. 960 ml Dextrose 60% in water

11. Determine the volume needed if the flow rate is 130 ml per hour and it will continuously run over 24 hours?

A. 1230 ml
B. 3000 ml
C. 3120 ml
D. 4000 ml

12. Determine the volume needed if the flow rate is 0.5L per hour and it will continuously run over 4 hours?

A. 1.2L
B. 2500 ml
C. 2000 ml
D. 0.125 L

13. A patient is on an infusion running at 500 ml per hour. The pharmacy has sent the nurse eight 1L bags. How long will it take to infusion?

A. 2 hours
B. 16 hours
C. 18 hours
D. 2000 ml

14. Order 25 mg to run over 4 hours. How much medication will the patient receive per hour?

 A. 6.25 mg/hour
B. 100 mg/ hour
C. 12.5 mg
D. 25 mg

15. The doctor ordered 100 mg /50 ml NaCl over 30 minutes. How much medication will the patient receive per hour?

A. 50 mg/hour
B. 100 mg/ hour
C. 150 mg/ hour
D. 200 mg/ hour

16. 6gm of active ingredient is mixed with 120gm of ointment base. What is the final concentration?

 A. 2%
B. 4.76%
C. 5%
D. 3%

17. 700mg of active ingredient is mixed with 40 gm of ointment base. What is the final concentration?

A. 2%
B. 1.5%
C. 1.7%
D. 3%

18. How much potassium chloride is contained in 1.2L of KCL 20% (w/v) solution?

A. 4.17gm
B. 417 gm
C. 215 mg
D. 240 gm

19. 6 oz of active ingredient to total 500ml of an alcohol-based solution. What is the final concentration? (v/v)

A. 24%
B. 0.79%
C. 26%
D. 36%

20. If you dilute 250ml of a 14% solution to 3.5%, how much could you produce?

A. 500ml
B. 1000ml
C. 0.196 ml
D. 62.5ml

21. How much chlorpromazine 250 mg/ml should you dilute to prepare 750 ml of chlorpromazine 25mg/ml?

A. 75ml
B. 7500ml
C. 8.3 ml
D. 83ml

22. What is the flow rate to be used to infusion 1200 ml of dextrose 5% in water over 6 hours if the set delivers 15 drops per ml?

A. 25 gtts/min
B. 50 gtts/min
C. 75 gtts/min
D. 90 gtts/min

23. Doctor orders Cefepime 1gm tid. The drug is available as a 500 mg/5ml vial. What volume should be given for each dose?

A. 4ml
B. 6ml
C. 8ml
D. 10ml

24. What volume of a 4% Hydrocortisone solution can be made from 45gm of Hydrocortisone powder?

A. 750 ml
B. 1000ml
C. 1125ml
D. 1500ml

25. How many 100 mg tablets would be required to make 1.2 liters of a 1:500 solution?

A. 24 tablets
B. 30 tablets
C. 42 tablets
D. 60 tablets

26. The recommended dose of Cefadroxil is 30 mg/kg/day. What would be the daily dosage for a child who weighs 50 kg?

A. 600mg
B. 681.2mg
C. 1500mg
D. 3300mg

27. Vitamin E capsule cost $7.99 for a 100-count bottle. If a patient with no insurance comes in with a discount card for 30% off the price plus a $0.75 dispensing fee, what is the selling price?

A. $2.40
B. $6.34
C. $3.15
D. $7.24

28. How many tablespoons are in 128 oz?

A. 96 tablespoons
B. 144 tablespoons
C. 256 tablespoons
D. 384 tablespoons

29. Convert the following number to Roman numerals: 1761

A. MCMXXVII
B. MDCLVII
C. MDCCLXVII
D. MDCCLXI

30. The term antitussive refers to:

A. Relieves itching
B. Relieves hives
C. Reduce swelling
D. Relieves coughing

31. Analgesic drugs are to pain relief, as antipyretic drug is to:

A. Relieves hives
B. Reduce fevers
C. Raise heart rate
D. Relieves coughing

32. Change the following ratio to a percentage: 7: 82

A. 7%
B. 8%
C. 9%
D. 10%

33. Convert the following to an Arabic number: MMCDLIV

A. 2544
B. 2454
C. 2684
D. 2554

34. Rx: Prednisone 10 mg tablets: 1-tab po tid x 3 days, 1-tab po bid x 3 days, 1-tab po qd x 3 days. What is the total medication needed in tablets and in mg?

A. 18 tablets, 180 mg
B. 180 tablets, 10 mg
C. 20 tablets, 360 mg
D. 360 tablets, 20 mg

35. The process that brings a drug to it "first pass" and makes a drug inactive is called?

A. Absorption
B. Distribution
C. Metabolism
D. Excretion

36. The prescribers DEA number is needed for what type of prescriptions?

A. C-II only
B. Anabolic Steroids
C. C-II through C-V
D. When ordering controls from a wholesaler

37. The federal health insurance provided to people age 65 and over is called:

A. Medicaid
B. Medicare
C. Blue Cross Blue Shield
D. United Health

38. The process that brings a drug from the route of administration site into the bloodstream is called:

A. Absorption
B. Distribution
C. Metabolism
D. Excretion

39. You have Solu-Medrol 40mg/2ml. The dose needed is 7.2 ml. How many mg will be administered?

A. 11.1 mg
B. 144 mg
C. 111 mg
D. 0.36 mg

40. The abbreviation for Kidney is:

A. Nephr/o
B. Hepat/o
C. Kidn/o
D. Rhin/o

41.The root word for Nose is:

A. Pyr/o
B. Itis
C. Rhin/o
D. Nasal

42. The Latin abbreviation for "right ear" is:

A. UD
B. AD
C. AS
D. OS

43. The Latin abbreviation for "both eyes" is:

A. OU
B. AD
C. AS
D. OS

44. 14 grains is the same as how many mg?

A. 840 mg
B. 868 mg
C. 916 mg
D. 882 mg

45. The common stem ending -Pril is for what classification:

A. Beta Blockers
B. Alpha Blockers
C. Oral Contraceptive
D. Ace Inhibitors

46. If a person weighs 178 kg, how many pounds does that person weigh?

A. 392 lbs.
B. 81 lbs.
C. 392 lbs.
D. 445 lbs.

47. Which chemical symbol represents Sodium?

A. S
B. Sd
C. Na
D. H

48. What is 65% of 84?

A. 15
B. 23
C. 1.29
D. 54.6

49. A solution is labeled as 1: 4678. What is the percentage strength of the solution?

A. 0.025%
B. 0.021%
C. 0.25%
D. 0.55%

50. Convert 0.2 mg to grain:

A. 1/12 gr
B. 1/150 gr
C. 1/250 gr
D. 1/300 gr

51. The abbreviation for "under the tongue" is:

A. SL
B. SC
C. UD
D. SD

52. Another name for Sodium Chloride is:

A. 0.9%
B. Normal Saline
C. NaCl
D. All the above

53. 14 liter is the same as _____ oz.

A. 128
B. 14000
C. 467
D. 30

54. You have Amoxicillin 250 mg / 5ml and need to dispense a 276mg dose. How many ml are needed?

A. 4 ml
B. 5.5 ml
C. 6.2 ml
D. 55.2ml

55. The Pharmacy Manager just called the local DEA office and local police about the stolen Ritalin tablets. What form should the Pharmacy Manager send to the DEA?

A. DEA Form 41

B. DEA Form 106
C. DEA Form 222
D. DEA Form 224

56. At what temperature should Zoster be stored?

A. 2*C to 8*C
B. 20*C to 56*C
C. -58*F to 5*F
D. 32*F to 46*F

57. This eye drop is stored in the refrigerator before it is dispensed to patients:

A. Timolol
B. Olopatadine
C. Latanoprost
D. Brimonidine

58. Once Insulin is removed from the refrigerator and opened, it has an expiration date of:

A. 14 days
B. 21 days
C. 28 days
D. 30 days

59. This level IOS is the dirtiest of them all, but cleaner than most normal room atmospheres:

A. IOS 1
B. IOS 5
C. IOS 8
D. IOS 9

60. The pressure in an IOS 8 clean room must be _____ and has _____ air changes:

A. Positive, 13
B. Negative, 20
C. Positive or Negative, 25
D. No pressure, No changes

61. Schedule 2 prescriptions have an expiration date of:

A. 1 calendar year
B. 90 days
C. 60 days
D. 30 days

62. Non-controlled substance drugs can have a total of _____ refills.

A. 0 refills
B. 5 refills
C. 6 refills
D. 11 refills

63. When a patient wants a brand name drug, and the physician allows the substitution with generic drug, what DAW code should be used?

A. DAW 1
B. DAW 2
C. DAW 3
D. DAW 0

64. When the brand name drug is mandated by law, what DAW code should be used?

A. DAW 7
B. DAW 5
C. DAW 9
D. DAW 4

65. What DAW is used when no generic is available at the pharmacy and the patient is allowed to get the brand name at the generic price?

A. DAW 7
B. DAW 6
C. DAW 5
D. DAW 4

66. A 3-Filing System in a retail pharmacy is a filing system that has:

A. All the controlled prescription bundled together
B. Only the non-controlled medications and C-III through C-V are bundled together
C. C-II, C-III through C-V, and non-controlled prescriptions are bundled separately
D. 3-filling system are only used in institutional pharmacies

67. The green copy of the DEA Form 222 goes to who?

A. The pharmacy from the DEA
B. The wholesaler from the seller
C. The local DEA from the seller
D. The pharmacy from the wholesaler

68. This form is needed to operate as a controlled substance abuse treatment program or compound-controlled substance medications.

A. IOS 1
B. DEA Form 224
C. USP 797
D. DEA Form 363

69. If a pharmacy wishes to file all controlled substances into one bundle, all the C-III through C-V prescriptions must have a red letter "C" stamped on the lower right-hand corner of the prescription. The second bundle will only contain legend/ non-controlled prescriptions in its bundle. What filing system is this?

A. Two File System- right hand
B. Two File System- left hand
C. Two File System- red "C"
D. Three filing system

70. Pharmacy is notified that a drug has consistency issues with potency. The public does not need to be notified. The probability of serious harm is not likely and the effects with the drug may be temporary or reversible. What type of recall is this?

A. Schedule 1 recall
B. Class 2 recall
C. Schedule 2 recall
D. Class 3 recall

71. Each drug has its own National Drug Code number. Drugs that have the same name, but different strengths, will have the same match first three numbers in this segment. What segment is this?

A. Segment 1
B. Segment 2
C. Segment 3
D. Segment 4

72. Bottles that have a pill count of 1000 will have a package size code of:

A. 01
B. 03
C. 10
D. 100

73. How many mL of the 15% and 2.5% alcohol-based solution is needed to produce 460 ml of a 7.5% alcohol-based solution.

A. 100 ml of the 15% and 360 ml of the 2.5%
B. 214 ml of the 2.5% and 246 ml of the 15%
C. 184 ml of the 15% and 276 ml of the 2.5%
D. 450 ml of the 2.5% and 10 ml of the 15%

74. This type of health insurance provides medical insurance for physicians' visits and medical equipment?

A. Medicaid Louisiana
B. Medicare Part A
C. Medicare Part B
D. Medicare Advantage

75. Pills enter the body via the oral route of administration. Unlike pills, intravenous injection bypasses the mouth completely. But no matter the route of administration, all medications will end up in the bloodstream. Once in the bloodstream, this process starts to happen?

A. Absorption
B. Distribution
C. Metabolism
D. Excretion

76. A patient has an IV that is running 175 ml/hr. If the total volume is 2000 ml, how many hours will this bag infuse?

A. 9.7 hours
B. 11.4 hours
C. 0.75 hours
D. 7.65 hours

77. A child weighs 65 lbs. How many mg would be appropriate for the child, if the normal adult dose is 350 mg using Clark's Rule?

A. 140 mg
B. 150 mg
C. 160 mg
D. 170 mg

78. A 26-month-old child needs Tylenol. The normal adult dose is 160mg/5ml. What is the appropriate dose, in ml, for the child using Fried's Rule?

A. 0.90 ml
B. 0.88 ml
C. 0.86ml
D. 140 ml

79. A child weighs 92 lbs. How many mg would be appropriate for the child, if the normal adult dose is 1gm using Clark's Rule?

A. 620 mg
B. 0.88 mg
C. 885 mg
D. 60 mg

80. Rx: Amoxicillin 250 mg: Take 1 tablet by mouth tid for 10 days. What quantity should be dispensed?

A. 3 tablets
B. 10 tablets
C. 30 tablets
D. 60 tablets

81. How many air changes happen per hour in an IOS 5 atmosphere?

A. 360
B. 210
C. 60
D. 20

82. Total Parenteral Nutrition (TPN), antibiotic injections, eye drops, other infusions bags and syringes can be prepared in this type of room?

A. ISO 1
B. USP 797
C. ISMP 19
D. USP 795

83. The first letter in a DEA Number is the:

A. The first letter of the prescriber's name
B. The last letter of the prescriber's last name
C. The prescriber's professional title
D. The first letter of the hospital name

84. Convert 113*F into C

A. 45 *C
B. 171.4*C
C. 32*C
D. 15*C

85. Convert 85.4* C to F

A. 96*F
B. 154*F
C. 210.5*F
D. 185.7 *F

86. This root word is for "Bladder"?

A. Carcin/o
B. Cardi/o
C. Cyst/o
D. Vas/o

87. The prefix Brady- means:

A. Fast
B. Inside
C. Slow
D. Heart

88. The suffix –rrhea means:

A. Flowing discharge
B. Bursting of blood flow
C. Blood Condition
D. Hardening

89. Generic drug name is not commercially available (No Generic has been created), what DAW code is this?

A. DAW 9

B. DAW 6
C. DAW 8
D. DAW 5

90. The suffixes –sclerosis means:

A. Flowing discharge
B. Bursting of blood flow
C. Blood Condition
D. Hardening

91. 25000mcg converted to gm

A. 0.25 gm
B. 0.025 gm
C. 2.5 gm
D. 25 gm

92. 175 gm converted to mg

A. 17500 mg
B. 1750 mg
C. 175000 mg
D. 17.5 mg

93. 176 tsp converted to gallon

A. 12 gal
B. 0.229 gal
C. 1 gal
D. 0.687 gal

94. In what proportion should 10% ethanol be mixed with 65% ethanol to obtain 50% ethanol with a volume of 330ml?

A. 9/10 of the 10% and 1/10 of the 65%

B. 8/11 of the 65% and 3/11 of the 10%
C. 1/10 of the 65% and 9/10 of the 10%
D. 2/3 of the 65% and 1/3 of the 10 %

95. Which of the following is a valid DEA prescriber registration number?

A. BB2453161
B. BB2453162
C. BB2453163
D. BB2453619

96. The following DEA number is valid for Dr. Jeffery Brown: B03894561

A. True
B. False

$$3 + 9 + 5 = 17$$
$$8 + 4 + 6 = 18$$

97. Every pharmacy is required to complete controlled substance inventory every:

A. Every month
B. Every 6 months
C. Annually
D. Bi-Annually

98. Inventory files are to be kept on hand for:

A. 1 year
B. 2 years
C. 4 years
D. 7 years

99. Vaccine should be stored at what temperature?

A. 36*F to 46* F
B. -5*C to 5*C
C. 0*C to 15*C
D. -5*F to 5*F

100. Prescriber order Ciprofloxacin 600mg/ 200 ml IVPB to run at a rate of 40ml/hr. If this infusion is hung at 10:30 am, at what time will this infusion be complete?

A. 5 hours
B. 3:30 pm
C. 10:30 pm
D. 5:00 am

101. A patient is to receive 65 units of insulin. The vial is labeled 50 units per 2 ml. How many ml will the patient need?

A. 2.1 ml
B. 2.3 ml
C. 2.6 ml
D. 2.8 ml

102. A patient is to receive 35 units of insulin. The vial is labeled 100 units per 1 ml. How many ml will the patient need?

A. 0.035ml
B. 0.35 ml
C. 3 ml
D. 3.5 ml

103. If a patient needs to receive 56 ml of a medication, how many oz will that be?

A. 1.9 oz
B. 1.8 oz
C. 1.7 oz
D. 1 oz

104. D5W means dextrose 5% in water. How many grams of dextrose is present in 100 ml?

A. 0.5 grams
B. 5 grams
C. 50 grams
D. 500 mg

105. NaCl 0.9% means Sodium Chloride 0.9%. How many mg of sodium chloride is present in 100 ml?
A. 0.9 mg
B. 9 mg
C. 90 mg
D. 900 mg

106. A drug is ordered at 500 mg IV q6h. When 20 ml of dilutant is added to 5gm vial, what is the concentration of each ml?
A. 100 mg/ ml
B. 200 mg/ ml
C. 250 mg/ ml
D. 4mg/ml

107. Use the concentration from question 106, how many ml will be needed to fill the medication order 500 mg IV q6h?

A. 2 ml
B. 4 ml
C. 6 ml
D. 8 ml

108. The prescriber has ordered 0.6 gm of a medication. The pharmacy has a supply of 300 mg tablets. How many tablets will the patient need?

A. 500 tablets
B. 2 tablets
C. 20 tablets
D. 100 tablets

109. Heparin 25,000 units/250 ml and the patient needs to receive 15,000 units. If the drop factor is 60 gtts/min and the IV will run for 100 ml/ hour, how many ml will the patient need for their dose?

A. 2 hours
B. 150 ml
C. 416 ml
D. 15000 gtts

110. Rx: Albuterol Inhaler 17.5gm: Inh 2 pf po tid Dispense: 1 device (200 puffs). What is the day supply?

A. 17 days
B. 30 days
C. 33 days
D. 34 days

111. Using the signa code from question 110, how many puffs would the patient take per day?

A. 2 puffs
B. 3 puffs
C. 6 puffs
D. 8 puffs

112. Using the signa code from question 110, how many doses would the patient have?

A. 33.3 doses
B. 100 doses
C. 66.7 doses
D. 66 doses

113. What is the flow rate to be used to infusion 200 ml of dextrose 5% in water over 4 hours, if the set delivers 60 drops per ml?

A. 40 gtts/min
B. 50 gtts/min
C. 75 gtts/min
D. 90 gtts/min

114. What is the flow rate to be used to infusion 2500 ml of dextrose 5% in water over 5.3 hours if the set delivers 30 drops per ml?

A. 235 gtts/min

B. 443 gtts/min

C. 236 gtts/min

D. 358 gtts/min

115. What is the flow rate to be used to infusion 120 ml of dextrose 10% in water over 3 hours if the set delivers 10 drops per ml?

A. 5 gtts/min

B. 6 gtts/min

C. 7 gtts/min

D. 36 gtts/min

116. A patient is on an infusion running at 50 ml per hour. The pharmacy has sent the nurse 2L bags. How long will it take to infusion?

A. 2 hours

B. 16 hours

C. 18 hours

D. 40 hours

117. A patient is on an infusion running at 750 ml per hour. The pharmacy has sent the nurse 4-liter bags. How long will it take to infusion?

A. 5 hours

B. 6 hours

C. 8 hours

D. 20 hours

118. This level IOS is the cleanest of them all:

A. IOS 1

B. IOS 5

C. IOS 8

D. IOS 9

119. Prescriber order Ciprofloxacin 600mg/ 200 ml IVPB to run at a rate of 40ml/hr. If this infusion is run over 6 hours, how many mg per hour will be infused?

A. 50 mg/ hour
B. 100 mg/ hour
C. 200mg/ hour
D. 600 mg/ hour

120. Prescriber order Azithromycin 125 mg tablet tid. Available is 250 mg tablets. If the day supply is 7 days, how many tablets should be dispensed?

A. 10 tablets

B. 11 tablets

C. 7 tablets

D. 14 tablets

121. 1 pint is equal to _____ tbsp.

A. 96 tbsp

B. 16 tbsp

C. 32 tbsp

D. 48 tbsp

122. 4410 ml is equal to _____ gal.

A. 1.15 gal

B. 1 gal

C. 0.87 gal

D. 1.21 gal

123. 78 lbs. is equal to _____ gm

A. 35.5 gm

B. 35500 gm

C. 78000 gm

D. 34455 gm

124. Pataday eye drops are available in 15 ml. If each ml contains 20 gtts/ml, how many drops will the patient have?

A. 1.3 gtts

B. 900 gtts

C. 200 gtts

D. 300 gtt

125. Using the information from question 129, if the patient must Instill 2 gtts tid into each eye, what would be the day supply?

A. 20 days

B. 25 days

C. 30 days

D. 60 days

126. A patient prescription needs to have the following on it:

A. Date written

B. Date of birth

C. Drug name and quantity

D. All the above

127. The drug classification PPI means:

A. Protein package insert
B. Patient protein insert
C. Patient package insert
D. Protein pump inhibitors

128. The stem ending –Pam and –Lam belongs to this drug classification:

A. Benzodiazepine
B. Beta Blocker
C. Macrolide
D. Laxative

129. The stem ending –zosin belongs to this drug classification:

A. Angiotensin II Receptor Blocker
B. Alpha Blocker
C. H2 Antagonist
D. HMG CoA Reductase Inhibitor

130. Calcium Channel Blockers are used to treat this:

A. Water retention
B. A-fib
C. Malarial
D. Gestational Hypertension

131. Local Anesthetic stem endings have the ending of:

A. -Tal
B. -Caine
C. -trop-
D. -conazole

132. Doxorubicin and Daunorubicin are examples of this type of medication:

A. Monoclonal Antibody Drug
B. Direct Thrombin Inhibitor
C. Antineoplastics Drug
D. PARP inhibitors

133. -Alol and Ilol are stem endings for this drug classification:

A. PPI
B. Beta Blocker and Alpha Blocker
C. Beta Blocker
D. Antiarrhythmic

134. Acyclovir and Valacyclovir are medications used to treat:

A. Herpes
B. Coronavirus
C. Chicken Pox
D. Monkey Pox

135. Fe is the chemical symbol for which of the following elements?

A. Sodium
B. Lead
C. Potassium
D. Iron

136. The Roman Numeral "ss" is used to represent what Arabic number?

A. 2
B. 1/2
C. 2000
D. 40

137. Ketoconazole and Fluconazole are examples of drugs used to treat this type of infection?

A. Bacterial
B. Viral
C. Fungal
D. Septic

138. If a medication is "ac", it will be taken:

A. before meal
B. Around the clock
C. After meals
D. With meals

139. If an insurance company pays for a 15 days supply and the prescription is for "i-ii caps po q6h", what is the maximum number of capsules that can be dispensed?

A. 56
B. 84
C. 120
D. 180

140. If an insurance company pays for a 30 days supply and the prescription is for "ii-iii tabs po tid", what is the maximum number of tablets that can be dispensed?
A. 30
B. 90
C. 180
D. 270

141. High blood sugar is known as:

A. Polyuria
B. Hypoglycemia
C. Sitagliptin
D. Hyperglycemia

142. Rhinoplasty is known as:

A. Surgical removal of the stomach
B. Surgical repair of the nose
C. Surgical removal of the kidneys
D. Surgical repair of the heart

143. The bolded section of the National Drug Code 64585-**0832-**10 identifies the:

A. Drug manufacturers
B. Drug name, strength, and dosage form
C. Package size
D. Both A and B

144. This type of Medicare pays for prescriptions only

A. Part A
B. Part B
C. Part C
D. Part D

145. Which of the following equals 46 tsp?

A. 690 ml
B. 1380 ml
C. 230 ml
D. 5520 ml

Answer Key

1	b	31	b
2	c	32	c
3	b	33	b
4	d	34	a
5	b	35	c
6	a	36	c
7	c	37	b
8	b	38	b
9	c	39	b
10	a	40	a
11	c	41	c
12	c	42	b
13	b	43	a
14	a	44	a
15	d	45	b
16	b	46	c
17	c	47	c
18	d	48	d
19	d	49	b
20	b	50	d
21	a	51	a
22	b	52	d
23	d	53	c
24	c	54	b
25	a	55	b
26	c	56	c
27	b	57	c
28	c	58	c
29	d	59	d
30	d	60	b

Answer Key

61	b	91	b	121	c
62	d	92	c	122	a
63	b	93	b	123	c
64	a	94	b	124	d
65	c	95	d	125	b
66	c	96	b	126	d
67	c	97	d	127	d
68	d	98	b	128	a
69	a	99	a	129	b
70	b	100	b	130	d
71	b	101	c	131	b
72	c	102	b	132	c
73	c	103	a	133	c
74	c	104	b	134	a
75	b	105	d	135	d
76	b	106	c	136	b
77	b	107	a	137	c
78	b	108	b	138	a
79	a	109	b	139	c
80	c	110	c	140	d
81	a	111	c	141	d
82	b	112	b	142	b
83	c	113	b	143	b
84	a	114	c	144	d
85	d	115	c	145	c
86	c	116	d		
87	c	117	a		
88	a	118	a		
89	c	119	b		
90	d	120	b		

(intended for notes)

(intended for notes)

(intended for notes)

(intended for notes)

(intended for notes)

(intended for notes)

(intended for notes)

(intended for notes)

(intended for notes)

(intended for notes)

(intended for notes)

Final Thoughts

"Why did you create this book?" Because I was not satisfied with having a this information scattered across several of notebooks. I was fed up with creating multiple worksheets and having three different tutoring packets for my Pharmacy Technician students. Creating this book was not easy (lo I literally revised my table of content page sixteen times. Every time I tutored my student: John Bell, CPhT; from Chicago, IL; I realized that I needed to add a new section in the book. I am thankful to my two sons, Mikal (14) and Israel (2) for being understanding about the long nights an microwaved meals. I hope to make them proud of me and everything I ar doing for pharmacy in America. With the information in this book, my current pass rate for the national exams are at 87%. Most of my student use this information and my tutoring services to assist in passing their national exam. I am located in New Orleans, Louisiana; but I have many students all across the United States, Canada, and Ghana. I hope this boc helps you along your journey to becoming a Certified Pharmacy Technicia I wish you much success on your journey. Good Luck!!!

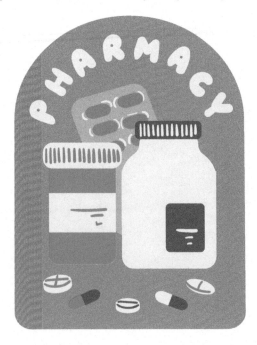

Made in the USA
Coppell, TX
20 March 2023

14482018R00046